Table of Contents

Thank you for purchasing **Scrapbooking Through the Year**, published by Creative Concepts. Other publications by Creative Concepts include **200 Great Scrapbook Layout Ideas** and **200 MORE Great Scrapbook Layout Ideas**. All three books are great resources for the scrapbook hobbyist. Our publications are designed for the beginner as well as the experienced scrapbook hobbyist. Some of the ideas in our books are simple and can be completed quickly, while others are more complex and may take many hours to complete. No matter what your scrapbook experience may be, we hope you will enjoy this book and will share it with a friend!

Creative Concepts wants to express our deepest appreciation for the many talented artists who submitted ideas for this book. We are fortunate to be in an industry with so many creative people. The success of Creative Concepts has been a wonderful blessing from God, for which we are thankful. We also thank our friends and customers for the prosperity of our company and hope you enjoy all our publications.

To order, please contact your local scrapbook store, distributor or:
Creative Concepts
Ph/fax# 256-350-9994 / Website: www.scrapbookingideas.com
Email: creativeconcepts@scrapbookingideas.com

Graphic services by:
Murphree Designs of Decatur, AL - www.rivercityadvertising.com
Dixie Graphics of Decatur, AL - Email: dixieg@hiwaay.net

Winter

February 2000

This was Callahan's first experience with snow. He was so bundled up, he couldn't move.

"SNOW"
by Jennifer Blackham of West Jordan, UT

Letter stickers: Provo Craft Alphabities
Lettering template: Scrap Pagers
Snowflake punch: Marvy
Journaling: PC Whimsy; For Fonts Sake Hugware
Oval cutter: Coluzzle Provo Craft

"Having A Ball"
by Lana Rickabaugh of Maryville, MO

Journaling fonts: Cool Dots
Title font: Baby Kruffy
Paper: Provo Craft
Snowflakes: unknown

Phil, Seth and Tanner spend a late afternoon building a snow fort in the back yard. After weeks of on and off snow and very cold temps, it warmed up enough to make the snow sticky.

January 2001

HAVing A Ball

Landon loved being the "big brother" and teaching Callahan how to make a snowball. Hopefully, Callahan will learn to wear a coat and mittens when playing in the snow.   Brrr!

February 2001

Landon & Callahan
Blackham

"Snowball Boys"
by Jennifer Blackham of West Jordan, UT

Paper: Paper Adventures
Font: PC Whimsy; For Fonts Sake Hugware
Lettering template: Pebbles Serif
Vellum
Circle punches

Our First House

In March of 1995, we moved into our first new house. I remember when Grayson put up the mailbox with our name on it. Home Tweet Home!

"Home Tweet Home"
by Jennifer Blackham of West Jordan, UT

Journaling font: CK Script
Title font: PC Chunky Jumbled For Fonts Sake
Birdhouse die cuts: Heartland Paper Co.
Raffia
Cardstock

Valentine's Day

"Love Letter"
by Sherri Winstead of McChord AFB, WA

Vellum: Paper Adventures
Stickers: Jolee's Boutiques
Cardstock: Pebbles
Pen: American Crafts; Ultimate Gel
Lettering template: Pebbles in My Pocket
Font: Provo Craft Whimsy

"Sweet Love"
by Vivian Smith of Calgary Canada

Paper: Susan Branch
Envelope: Provo Craft, card and envelope Coluzzle
Font: Marydale; downloaded from internet
Title: own design

"Happy Anniversary"
by Traci Johnson of Mesa, AZ

Paper: Mulberry; majenta
Canford; gold
Stickers and title: Cock-A-Doodle Design
Pen: Pigma Micron .05 black
Scissors: Fiskars; Deckle
Decorative corners: 3L
Heart punch: Family Treasures

"Tweet-hearts"
by Linda Jones of Long Beach, CA

Pattern paper: Paper Loft
Cardstock: Pebbles in My Pocket
Button: Hillcreek Design
Lettering template: Pagerz-Party
Paper piecing Idea: from Sarah Klemish

"The Love of My Life"
by Vivian Smith of Calgary Canada

Paper: Canford; gold
Carolee's Creations; red
Wintech; suede
Cupid: downloaded from internet
Watercolor pencils: Prisma Color
Photo corners: Canson
Font: Loki cola, from internet
Journaling: CK Curlz

Valentine's Day

"I Love You To Mama"
by Catherine Allan
of Twin Falls, ID

Lettering template: Page
Grade School
Vellum: unknown
Eyelets: Impress Rubber
Stamps
Wire: Artistic Wire
Page accents: Bumper
Crops
Computer font: DJ Goo (
Inkers)
Tip: Tan cardstock was
sprayed with water,
crumpled up, spread back
out and used for the
lettering,
photo mats and borders

"Hearts"
by Lana Rickabaugh
of Maryville, MO

Hearts: Beary Patch
Burlap paper: Frances Meyer
Pop dots: All Night Media
Other: Buttons, jute

"Hunny Bunny"
by Traci Johnson of Mesa, AZ

Letter template: DJ Inkers
Pens: Pentel; milky pink, milky green,
metallic silver and Zig .5 black Writer
Velour paper: Vivelle
Bunny: original design

"What A Crack-up"
by Jennifer Blackham of West Jordan, UT

Title: Provo Craft; Headliners Hugware Clip Art
Paper: Provo Craft; That's My Baby Scrap Pad
Chick clip art: FrameLiners CD; PC Hugware
Font: For Fonts Sake Hugware

"High Flyin' Fun"
by Lana Rickabaugh of Maryville, MO

Paper: Frances Meyer
Lettering template: Provo Craft Blocky
Pop dots: All Night Media

"Butte'lful Day"
by Traci Johnson of Mesa, AZ

Lettering template:
EK. Success
Pen: Marvy Le Plume;
"mocha" fine tip

October
2000

Kelsey
at the
USU
Gardens

Springtime in Cache Valley!
Melissa   May 1998

"Kelsey in the Garden"
by Kiyoko Walkenhorst of Bluffdale, UT

Products are from Scrap in a Snap

"Springtime in Cache Valley"
by Kiyoko Walkenhorst of Bluffdale, UT

Stickers: Mrs. Grossman's
Pen: Pentel Milky Gel
Zig Writer; Denim
Bubble paper: unknown
Vellum: unknown

Tips: Clouds were embossed with a milky gel pen by tracing the shape with the vellum on a mouse pad. This gave a nice white line and embossed edges. Glue placement was chosen to give the clouds a shadow look. Cloud stickers were trimmed on two edges to fit the squares.

"Fragrant Summer Breezes"
by Kiyoko Walkenhorst of Bluffdale, UT

Paper and embellishments: Scrap In A Snap
Pen: Pentel Milky Gel
Deckle edge scissors: Backstreet
Font: Harrington, free download

It's the little touches of beauty in life that fascinate me.

Our neighbors planted flowers all along the ditch bank this spring. By late summer they were lush.

Melissa and Kelsey, August 1998

"Sweet Summertime"
by Natasha Roe
of Sebring, FL

Patterned paper: Making Memories
Solid paper: Northern Sky
Pen: Micron
Font: DJ Squirrelly (modified)

"YUM"
by Jennifer Blackham of West Jordon, UT

Patterned paper: Provo Craft
Lettering template: PC Blocky
Letter stickers: Provo Craft Alphabitties
Watermelon diecuts: Heartland Paper Co.

> A hot August afternoon gave way to some wet and wild cooling off for Bryce and Elise. Bryce was more than willing to get wet and get anyone withing hosing distance wet, but Elise was a little more reserved, opting instead for the drink-from-the-hose method. August, 1998

"Summer Time"
by Catherine Allan
of Twin Fall, ID

Cardstock: Bazill; Canary, White
Patterned paper: Stamping Station; Sweetwater
Buttons: LaPetite; Hill Creek
Daffodil Twistel: Making Memories
Fibers: Rub a Dub Dub
Chalk: Craf-T
Colored pencils: EK Success
Circle punches: Family Treasures, Emaginations
Computer fonts: Marydale; downloaded from the internet,
CK Simplicity from the Art of Creative Lettering CD

"Fun in the Sun"
by Cindy Harris of Brentwood, CA

Cardstock: Making Memories
Pattern paper: Provo Craft
Vellum: Paper Adventure
Lettering template: Frances Meyer; Fat caps
Scissors: Fiskars Deco
Punch: Family Treasures, McGill, Splat
Pen: Zig Millennium; black

Tip: The title was made by cutting the blue papers with the deco edge scissors and placing them on white cardstock, one above the other with the white showing through. Then place your template right side up so you can see your placement of the waves and trace your title lightly with pencil. Cut out letters and erase any pencil lines. Place in a title block and add sun punch.

To make the punch art, punch a square from a large square punch in white, then again in the two blues and cut them in four halves. Place them inside the large white square punch with the white showing through partly and trim off the excess edges. Mat on green cardstock and trim. Add the sun punch in the middle.

"Summer"
by Melissa Fortenberry of Tuckerman, AR

Cardstock: Bazzill
Cut outs: Accent U Art
Paper: Fever Pattern Paper
Font: CK Journaling

"Snorkel"
by Dee Gallimore-Perry of Griswold, CT

Lettering template: Provo Craft; Blocky
Eyelet: Impress Rubber Stamps
Paperkin: EK Success
Computer font: CK Handprint
Patterned paper: Provo Craft; Color Wheel
Pen: Zig Millennium

Alec took to the river like a fish to the water. He had such a good time playing and pretending to swim in the cool water. I'm sure he will be really swimming before we know it. June 2001

July 2000
Brendan and Poppy in the pool! OK...so he might not be snorkeling at this moment...he's having too much fun riding on Poppy's back! But, when Poppy isn't in the water to play with, Brendan snorkels around and around and around! He does great! He rarely goes in the pool without his snorkel and mask on!
Maybe he'll be an underwater adventurer when he grows up?

"Swimming Lessons"

by Jami Blackham
of Portland, OR

Lettering stickers: Me & My Big
Ideas
Pen: Zig; Millennium Border
Templates: Colluzzle Circle and
Wave Splashes

EVERY SUMMER WE TOOK SWIM LESSONS AT THE CRESTWOOD POOL WITH THE NEIGHBORHOOD KIDS. THEN AFTER LESSONS WE WOULD EAT LUNCH WHILE WAITING FOR OPEN PLUNGE SO WE COULD SWIM SOME MORE.

GIGGLY GIRLS JACI SHELL, ME, JENNY APKING, JODI, AND LONNIE WILLIAMS
BEST BUDS JEREMY AND JASON APKING (AND ME!)

You are My Sunshine"

by Cindy Harris of Brentwood, CA
Cardstock: Westrim
Vellum: Paper Adventures
Rectangle punch: EK Success
Pens: Zig Millennium (Black), Zig Bullet Tip (Yellow)
Title font: CK Expedition

Tip: Mat photo on white cardstock. Use rectangle punch (or a square punch cut in half) to make the design around the photo. Cut away the white mat following the pattern from the rectangles. Mat on turquoise and yellow cardstock. The title was made by printing it on paper, then tracing with a black pen onto vellum. When dry, fill in with yellow

"Bathing Beauties"

by Cindy Harris of Brentwood, CA

Cardstock: Making Memories
Two tone cardstock (orange torn): Paper Adventures
Punches: McGill; large square, Family
Treasures; sun, EK Success; small square and rectangle
Lettering template: Chatterbox
DMC embroidery floss
Needle: Dritz
Pen: Zig Millennium

Analisa + Analisa · May 200?

"Let's Water Ski - Not"
by Vivian Smith of Calgary Canada

Font: CK Journaling, The Best of Creating Keepsakes Lettering, vol. 3 casual, downloaded from the internet
Circle cutter: Provo Craft Circle Coluzzle
Sun, Water, clouds: own design
Other: tissue paper

"Lighthouse"
by Jeanette Brinkerhoff
of Salt Lake City, UT

Patterned paper: Cloud - Karen Foster
Cardstock: red, navy, pastel blue light, pastel blue med, white
Pens: Zig Writer; red, black
Gel Pens; white
Fonts: CK Script
Lighthouse: Scrapping by Alaine.com
Sailboat: adapted from Provo Craft Template
Chalks: Stampin Up!

Tip: The journaling is the lyrics from my favorite song by Garth Brooks.

"Beach Bum"
by Cindy Harris
of Brentwood, CA

Cardstock: Making Memories
Beach Bum die cut: Stamping Station
Vellum: Paper Adventures
Pen: Zig Millennium
Button: Dress it Up
Star fish: Bought at the Wharf
Sticks: Found in the dried floral department of the local craft store
Chalk: Craf-T

Tip: The die cut letters are accented with layered torn cardstock. Brown torn cardstock is used for the hill and hand cut grass is used to accent.

"By The Sea"

by Lisa Miller of Austin, TX

Cardstock: Paper Garden
Paper piecing pattern: Bumper
Crops Idea Book I
Chalk: Craf-T

Journaling: CK Combo Font; cursive
"Sand" paper: unknown
Pen: EK Success
Anchor rope and white ribbon: unknown

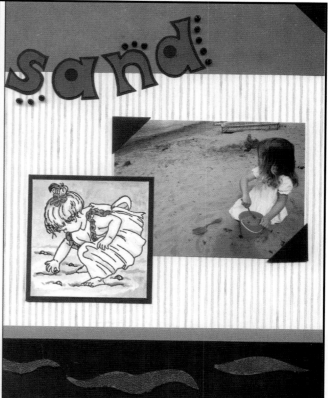

Sage enjoys playing at the beach by Sharon's cabin. It is one of the few areas that has sand. The lakeside by our cabin is mostly rocks, although a load of sand is occasionally dumped on the shore.

"Sun & Sand"

by Vivian Smith of Calgary Canada

Paper: Susan Branch
Letter template: Provo Craft
Stamp: Hero
Embossing powder: Creative Zoo
Water color pencils: Prisma Color
Font: Marydale, downloaded from the internet

Paper pieced deer: own design
Fish punch: unknown
Pail and Shovel: Provo Craft Beach Template
Sun: Made with a Provo Craft Circle Coluzzle
Font: Word Perfect; Technical

Deer Creek"
by Jennifer Blackham of West Jordan, UT

Tip: In order to over lap the photos on the left page, without covering anyone in the photos, I silhouetted my husband's head with an X-acto knife and then pulled it to the front.

"Solo Point Beach"
by Sherri Winstead of McChord AFB, WA

Stickers: Jolee's Boutiques
Pebbles/stones: Ek Success Camping
Tracerkin; traced and cut out
Blue vellum: Paper Adventures
Pebbles: cardstock

Tip: The pebbles and stones were adhered with pop dots for added dimension.

This layout includes two mini-scrapbooks
with photos inside.

"Half-Mast Hearts"
by Traci Johnson of Mesa AZ

Letter template: EK Success
Mini book templates: The Mini Scrapbook Kit
Decorative paper: Paper Patch and Frances Meyer
Laser die cuts: Deluxe Cuts
Letter stickers: Making Memories
Circle cutter: Creative Memories
Pen: Pigma Micron .05 black

"Aerobella"
by Traci Johnson of Mesa AZ

Eyelets: Dritz
Colored pencils: Prisma Color
Computer fonts: Creating Keepsakes;
Anything Goes and Bella

"America"
by Lana Rickabaugh of Maryville, MO

Star paper: Paper Patch
Header: Overalls
Gel Pen: Marvy

"4th"
by Lana Rickabaugh of Maryville, MO

Font: DJ Jenn Penn
Title: Provo craft template
Star punches: unknown
Pop dots: All Night Media
Large stars: hand cut

"Big Pile"
by Dee Gallimore Perry of Griswold, CT

Lettering template: Deja View; 2" Spunky
Better Letters
Cut outs: Cock-A-Doodle Design
Computer font: Scrap Simple; Inspire Graphic
Lettering Delights 2
Patterned paper: Mustard Moon
Pop dots: All Night Media
Pen: Zig Millennium

"Fall"
by Lana Rickabaugh of Maryville, MO

Lettering template: Provo Craft Blocky
Leaves: Black Ink
Paper: unknown
Hemp rope

"UnbeLEAFably Cool"
by Sherri Winstead of McChord AFB, WA

Leaves: Black Ink
Wacky Lettering
Template: EK Success
Fonts: CK Skinny Serif,
CK Jot
Cardstock: Pebbles
Pattern paper: Paper
Patch
Paper: unknown

"Autumn"
by Jami Blackham of Portland, OR

Title font: Gilligan; from the internet
Journaling font: Girls Are Weird; from the internet
Leaf punch: unknown
Paper: unknown

"Hayride"
by Dee Gallimore Perry of Griswold, CT

Wire: Create A Craft
Leaf punch: Family Treasures
Computer font: CK Handprint
Lettering template: Provo Craft Blocky

Tip: This idea includes gold wire to add a touch of pizzaz to a simple layout. Just wrap the wire around the square with the leaf punch.

Seth had so much fun in the leaves, until he fell in them. It was so funny because he would not get up by himself. I just laughed, lifted him up and sent him on his way again. Nov 2001

"Fall"
by Sherri Winstead of
McChord AFB, WA

Mini buttons: Dress it Up
Title and embellishments: Cock-A-Doodle
Page Pals
Pattern paper: Provo Craft
Font: Lettering Delights Mixed (LD Mixed)
CK Primary

We enjoyed the fall colors at Immigration Canyon. Sept 2000

"Autumn"
by Kiyoko Walkenhorst of Bluffdale, UT

Letter template: Provo Craft Blocky
Die cuts: Ellison
Paper: Scrap In A Snap

"Bed of Leaves"
by Sherri Winstead of
McChord AFB, WA

Font: DJ Jumble (DJ
Inkers)
Punches: Martha
Stewart Maple Leaf
Punch
Chalk: Craf-T
Jute
Vellum: Whispers
Autumn Leaves
Pop Dots

One of the nicest beds I know
isn't a bed of soft white snow,
isn't a bed of cool green grass
after the noisy mowers pass,
isn't a bed of yellow hay
making me itch for half a day—
but autumn leaves in a pile that high,
deep, and smelling like fall, and dry.
That's the bed where I like to lie
and watch the flutters go by.

Fall

"Autumn Memories"
by Briana Dziekan of Milford, MI

Eyelets
Gold powder: Jacquard Products
Brown cardstock
Paper: K & Company
Punches in shaker: Paper Shapers
Vellum: unknown
Title template: Chatterbox

The poem:
Autumn winds begin to blow;
Colored leave fall fast and slow.
Twirling, whirling all around.
Till at last, they touch the ground.
-author unknown

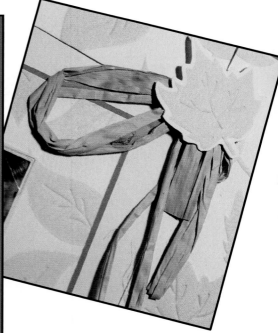

"Raffia"
by Kiyoko Walkenhorst of Bluffdale, UT

Paper: K & Company
Raffia

"Fall"
*by Catherine Allan
of Twin Fall, ID*

Patterned paper:
unknown
Mulberry: unknown
Lettering template:
Frances Meyer Fat
Letters
Eyelets: Impress
Rubber Stamps
Computer font: DJ
Dash
Other: Raffia

"Football"
by Briana Dziekan of Milford, MI

Leaf paper: Carolee's Paper
Brown striped paper: Pixie Press
Brown and tan cardstock
Pop dots
Title template: Chatterbox

"The Pumpkin Patch"

by Briana Dziekan of Milford, MI

Paper: Bo Bunny Press
Brown and green cardstock
Misc: eyelets and hemp
Page pieces: CADD
Pumpkin: own creation

"Pumpkin"

by Jennifer Blackham of West Jordan, UT

Paper: Bo Bunny
Topper and accents: My Minds Eye; Frame-Ups
Font: Cock-a-Doodle Design; Doodle Basic
vellum, cardstock, raffia and buttons

"In The Patch"
by Dee Gallimore Perry of Griswold, CT

Paper: Color Wheel Paper by Provo Craft
Computer fonts: Girls are Weird (internet), CK Toggle
Stickers: Provo Craft
Eyelets: Stamp Studio Inc.
Chalk: Craf-T Products

Tip: Place stickers onto torn white cardstock and chalk the edges. Use eyelets to attach to a coordinating cardstock. The same technique was used on the journaling block.

"Silly As A Scarecrow"
by Dee Gallimore Perry of Griswold, CT

Cut Outs: The Beary Patch
Chalk: Craf-T Products
Pen: Zig Millennium
Patterned paper: BoBunny Press; Fall Splatter
Computer font: CK Primary
Lettering template: Provo Craft; Blocky
Orange raffia: unknown source

"Boo from the Crew"
by Kristen Swain of Bear, DE

Font: CK Girl
Frame: My Mind's Eye
Cutouts: Beary Patch
Markers: Zig; black and gray
White Gel Pen: Uniball

"Too Cute To Spook"
by Lana Rickabaugh of Maryville, MO

Font: CK Chunky, CK Script
Diecut: unknown
Patterned "Boo" paper: unknown
Lavender Marvy Gel pen (background)

"Scary Faces...Spooky Places"
by Catherine Allan of Twin Falls, ID

Cardstock: Bazzill; black and pumpkin
Stickers: Sweetwater
Lettering template: Blocky (Provo Craft)
Eyelets: Impress Rubber Stamps
Vellum: unknown
Computer font: DJ Classic by DJ Inkers
Other: black grogain ribbon

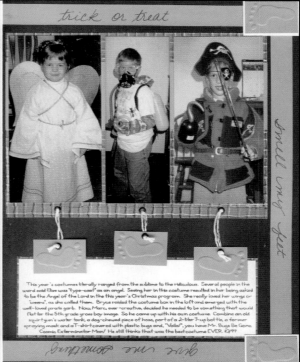

"Smell My Feet"
by Catherine Allan
of Twin Falls, ID

Printed paper: Provo Craft
Lettering template: Provo Craft; Blocky Large
Foot embossing template: Lasting Impressions
Eyelets: Impress Rubber Stamps
Computer fonts: CK Journaling
Title Feet: my own design

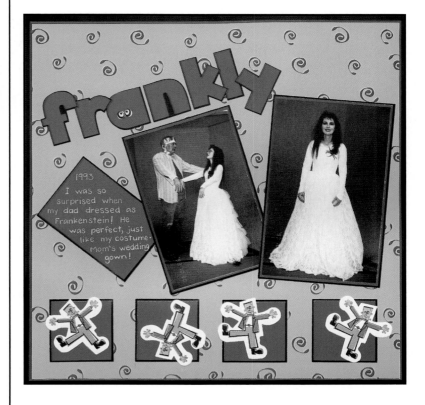

"Little Monster"
by Traci Johnson
Mesa, AZ

Letter template: DJ Inkers
Pens: Pentel; milky pink, milky green, metallic silver and Zig .5 black Writer
Velour paper: Vivelle
My original bunny paper piecing

"Frankly"
by Kiyoko Walkenforst
of Bluffdale, UT

Template: PC Blocky Lower
Eyes: punched from skeleton die cut
Papers & embellishments: Scrap in a Snap

Christmas

"Wisemen & Angels"
by Catherine Allan of Twin Falls, ID

Patterned papers: Robin's Nest
Embossed paper: unknown
Gold vellum: unknown
Chalk: Craf-T
Star punches: Marvy Uchida
Corner rounder: Marvy Uchida
Paper piecing patterns: 2 Peas in a Bucket
Computer fonts: CK Swirl
Journaling: CK Pretty
Largest Star: My own design. It was cut from gold
vellum, layered and chalked with black chalk.

"Christmas Is..."
by Jennifer Blackham of West Jordan, UT

Font: Inspire Graphic; Scrap Casual
Star punch: Family Treasures
Black pen: Millennium
Paper Piecing: Based on a tole painting design by Lisa
Ovsley of Clear Creek Creations

Tip: It is very easy to adapt tole painting patterns, coloring
books, clipart, stamps, etc. into a custom paper piecing for
your pages. Just copy (reduce or enlarge depending on the
size you need) and cut apart the pieces for your pattern.

"Christmas Joy"
by Lisa Goodman of Austin, TX

Cardstock: Paper Garden
Metallic paper and vellum: Paper Adventures
Jewels and sequins: unknown
Ribbon: Priced So Right
Letter stencil: unknown
Journaling: DJ Inkers Fancy Font

Tip: The idea came from the girls shirt, and sequins were used to fill in the blank area on the page. Pop dots were used to add dimension to the title.

"Cecilia's Family Christmas"
by Lisa Goodman of Austin, TX

Stencil title letters: Varsity Letters; Alpha Better Letters TCW9
Star punches and folk heart: Emagination
Pompom punch: EK Success; Thumb Punch
Computer font: CK Combo
Small heart punch: Fiskars

Tip: I punched and chalked small squares to give the look I wanted for the bottom checker border.

"Tis The Season"
by Briana Dziekan of Milford, MI

Green and tan cardstock
Pattern paper: unknown
Christmas squares: EK Success

"The Perfect Tree"
by Michelle Tardie of Richmond, VA

Title font: Wiffles; downloaded from
the internet
Cardstock: Bazzill Basics
Tree and start rub-ons: Provo Craft

"Christmas Joy"
by Kristen Swain
of Bear, DE

Font: CK Floozy
Punch: McGill Square
Handheld punch
Star punch: Paper
Shapers
Pen: Zig Black
Photo oil: Marshall

"Ho Ho Ho Lights"
by Traci Johnson of Mesa, AZ

Decorative scissors: Fiskars
Pen: Zig .5 black Millennium
Paper: Paper Pizzaz; "Tea Bag Scrapbooking" paper

"Christmas Cuties"
by Lana Rickabaugh of Maryville, MO

Paper: Paper Patch
Stickers: Mrs. Grossman
Gel pen: Marvy

"Mommy, Baby, Tummy!"

Dal & I thought it would be great to have our children about 3yrs apart. We didn't want their birthdays too close, so March 2001 seemed like an ideal time. I took a pregnancy test on August Fri. morning before I went to work & it came back positive. Since Dal is usually sleeping when I go to work, I left the house without telling him the exciting news. We had planned to meet at MEC after work that day. The entire time we were there, I kept the news to myself. Just as we were leaving, I asked Dal to stay inside while Sage & I went outside. I told Sage the exciting news & when Dal came outside, Sage exclaimed "Mommy, baby, tummy!". All Dal could say was "WOW!".

⊞ Pregnancy Differences ⊞

Felt more confident as to what to expect during the pregnancy.

Was sick once (with Sage I wasn't sick at all)

Had tons of cravings (had none the first time)

Didn't feel pregnant at first. With Sage I just knew I was.

Weeks went much faster with the 2nd pregnancy

Started showing at 6 weeks instead of 3 months

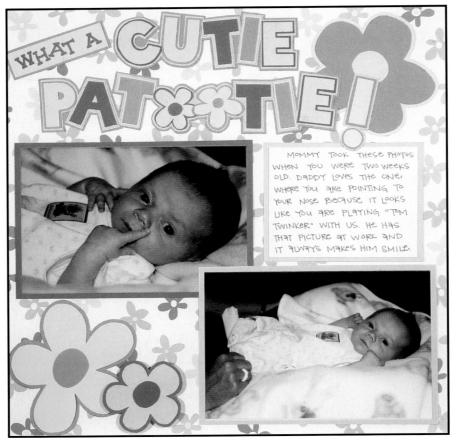

WHAT A CUTIE PATOOTIE!

MOMMY TOOK THESE PHOTOS WHEN YOU WERE TWO WEEKS OLD. DADDY LOVES THE ONE WHERE YOU ARE POINTING TO YOUR NOSE BECAUSE IT LOOKS LIKE YOU ARE PLAYING "TOM TWINKER" WITH US. HE HAS THAT PICTURE AT WORK AND IT ALWAYS MAKES HIM SMILE.

"Mommy, Baby, Tummy"
by Vivian Smith of Calgary Canada

Paper: Provo Craft (purple green in title)
Carolee's Creations (soft purple)
Font: Lumparsky (journaling)
PC Chunky; Provo Craft hugware, "It's a Wonderful Life"
Stickers: Sandy Lion
Stamp: Hero
Other: jute

"Cutie Patootie"
by Jami Blackham of Portland, OR

Paper: Royal Stationery; Rainboworld
Letter stickers: Provo Craft Alphabitties
Letter template: Pebbles In My Pocket
Pen: Zig Millennium

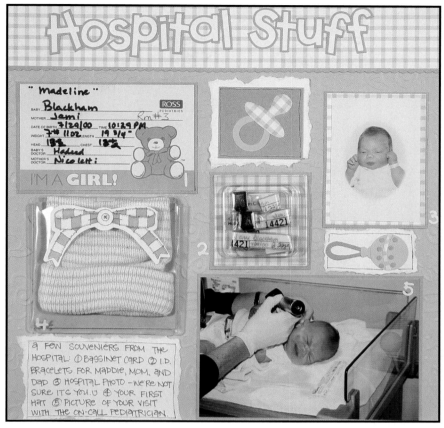

"Hospital Stuff"
by Jami Blackham of Portland, OR

Memorabilia pocket: 3L
Memorabilia box: Deja Views
Bow accent: O'Scraps
Letter stickers: Stickopotamus and Provo Craft
Patterned and embossed Paper: Frances Meyers
Baby micro template: Provo Craft
Scissors: Provo Craft; Scalloped

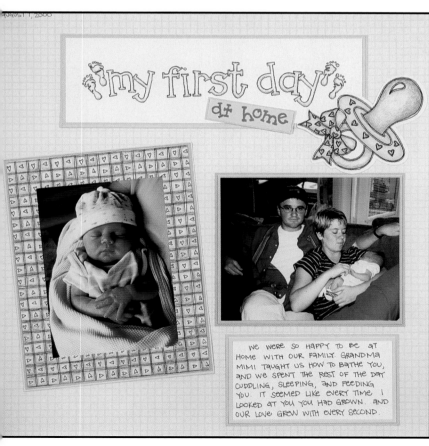

"My First Day"
by Jami Blackham of Portland, OR

Page topper: Cock-A-Doodle Design
Frame and die cut: O'Scrap
Letter stickers: Provo Craft Alphabitties
Pen: Zig Millennium
Paper: Imaginations

"Briana"
by Briana Dziekan of Milford, MI

Embossed paper: Royal Stationary
Patterned paper: Colorbok
Template: ABC Tracers
Doll with bed: Stamping Station

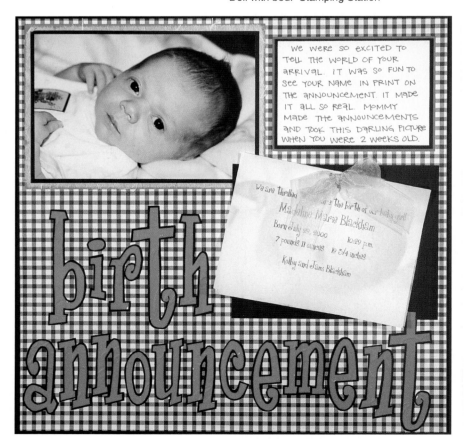

We were so excited to tell the world of your arrival. It was so fun to see your name in print on the announcement. It made it all so real. Mommy made the announcements and took this darling picture when you were 2 weeks old.

"Birth Announcement"
by Jami Blackham of Portland, OR

Font: Girls Are Weird; from the internet
Mulberry paper: Personal Stamp Exchange
Background paper: Frances Meyer
Pen: Zig Millennium
Embossed paper: Frances Meyer
Vellum: Staedtler

"Big Brother"
by Kiyoko Walkenhorst of Bluffdale, UT

All supplies: Scrap In A Snap

"Somebunny Special"
by Kristen Swain of Bear, DE

Cut-outs: Beary Patch
Patterned papers: KMA
Font: Scrap Baby
Jute

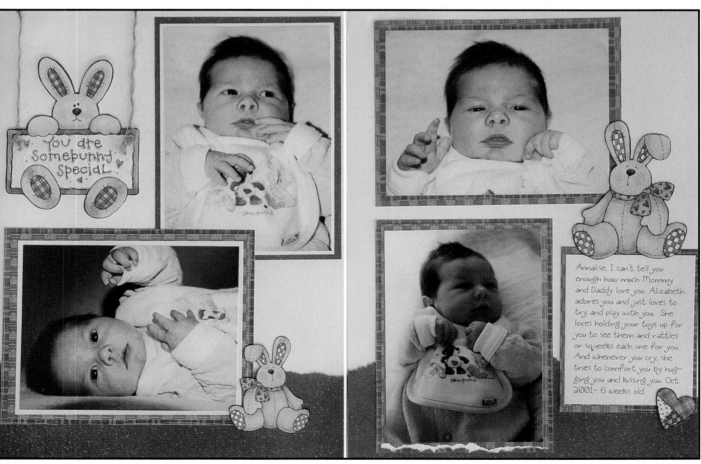

"She Fills Our Life With Sunshine"
by Kristen Swain of Bear, DE

Vellum: The Paper Company
Flower punch: Paper Shapers
Font: French Script

Tip: The pink paper was crumpled, dampened with water and allowed to dry.

"This Little Piggy"
by Jeanette Brinkerhoff of Salt Lake City, UT

Green Plaid Paper: KMA

Pink polk-a-dot paper: unknown
Cardstock: cream
Lettering templates: PC Scrapbook 1
Pens: Zig Writer, Gel Pens
Pigs: adapted from a craft shape of unknown source
Chalks: Stampin Up!
Other- Jute for pigs tails

"All Our Ducks In A Row"
by Jennifer Blackham of West Jordan, UT

Paper: Northern Spy
Lettering template: Pebbles Serif
Letter stickers: Provo Craft; Alphabitties
Font: Provo Craft; PC Whimsey

"Waddle I Do"
by Jeanette Brinkerhoff of Salt Lake City, UT

Paper: Northern Spy
Cardstock: white and dark yellow
Pens: Zig Writer, Gel Pens
Title: Die cut; unknown
Fonts: CK Bella
Paperpiecing Ducks: Handmade Scraps
Chalks: Stampin Up!

Note: These pages were submitted by Scrapcircle.com contestants using the same kits of cardstock, paper and matching embellishments. Even using the same supplies, the result is wonderfully different!

"Madeline Goes To Market"
by Jami Blackham of Portland, OR

Letter template: Frances Meyer
Pen: Zig Writers
Paper: Provo Craft

"Tub Time Fashions"
by Dee Gallimore Perry of Griswold, CT

Patterned paper: Doodlebug Designs
Beads and fibers: On The Surface
Buttons: Dress It Up
Craft thread: DMC
Computer fonts: Title -Love Letters; from the internet
Journaling: Inspired Graphics; Scrap Casual

"Blue Gingham"
by Jami Blackham of Portland, OR

Circle cutter: Provo Craft Colluzzle
Scissors: Fiskars, Mini Scallop
Pen: Zig Millennium
Flower punch: unknown
Circle punch: EK Success
Patterned paper: Paper Patch

"Sophie"
by Vivian Smith of Calgary Canada

Font: Carpenter; downloaded from the internet
Arial; Microsoft Word
CAC Pinafore
Ribbon: Fanny's Fabrics
Eyelet: Impress Rubber Stamp

"Maddie's Hat"
by Jami Blackham of Portland, OR

Letter stickers: Provo Craft
Patterned Paper: Provo Craft
Font: Provo Craft Childish

"Sheriff Karson"
by Jeanette Brinkerhoff of Salt Lake City, UT

Patterned paper: KMA; Red weave print
Cardstock: navy, green, kraft, cream
Title lettering templates: PC Scrapbook 1
Pens: Zig Writer; black, green
Gel Pens
Journaling: by hand
Bear head: adapted from Bear on baby's outfit

"Loves Me"
by Jami Blackham of Portland, OR

Pen: Zig Millennium
Overalls: EK Success
Scissors: Fiskars

Children

"My Artwork"
by Jennifer Blackham of West Jordan, UT

Paper: Frances Meyer
Title: Cock-A-Doodle Design
Font: DJ Crayon

"Artist in Training"
by Lana Rickabaugh of Maryville, MO

Paper: Sonburn
Sticker: Me and my Big Ideas
Fonts: CK cursive and Kids (downloaded from the internet)

"A Budding Artist"
by Anita Denson of Decatur, AL

Font: unknown
Red and blue cardstock
Crayons: own design

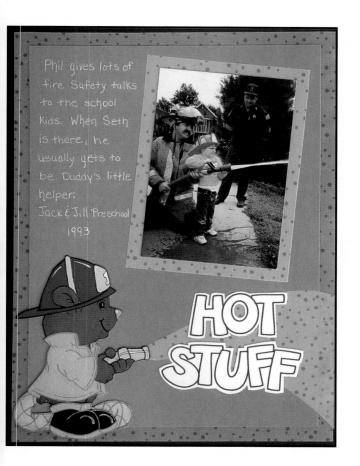

Phil gives lots of fire safety talks to the school kids. When Seth is there, he usually gets to be Daddy's little helper.
Jack & Jill Preschool
1993

HOT STUFF

FIRE SAFETY 101

Fireman Phil loves to go to visit the kids and give talks on fire safety. October is Fire Safety month so many trips are made to the local schools to teach the kids how to stop, drop and roll, to try on the turnout gear and also to show them how to escape from a burning house safely. Of course, no trip is complete without seeing Engine 3 or the fire dog Taz.
October 2000

MARYVILLE PUBLIC SAFETY ENG 3 INE

"Hot Stuff"
by Lana Rickabaugh of Maryville, MO

Font: CK Chunky
Gel Pen: Marvy
Vellum: unknown

"Fire Safety 101"
by Lana Rickabaugh of Maryville, MO

Title: CK Groovy
Font: CK Journaling
Punch people and dog: my own design

"Food and Fun"
by Jennifer Blackham of West Jordan, UT

Large letter stickers: Provo Craft Kids
Alphabitty letter stickers: Provo Craft Kids
Circle cutter: Coluzzle

FOOD and FUN!

Arctic Circle MaY '99

"Rainy Day"
by Dee Gallimore Perry of Griswold, CT

Topper, frames, cloud and umbrella cut outs: Cock-A-
Doodle Design
Patterned paper: Making Memories
Umbrella, clouds and drop stickers: Frances Meyer
Paperkins: EK Success
Pen: Zig Millennium
Computer font: CK Handprint
Letter A Sticker: Alphabitties by Provo Craft

Tip: This layout "pops" off the page using foam dots to
mount the umbrella and clouds.

"Rainy Days"
by Jennifer Blackham of West Jordan, UT

Letter stickers: Making Memories
Noah die cuts: Heartland Paper Co.
Font: CK Journaling
Umbrella: own design

"I'm A Lil' Ray of Sunshine"
by Lisa Miller of Austin, TX

Cardstock: Paper Garden
Stickers: Mrs. Grossman's
Punches: Square and Medium Circle;
Family Treasures, Small Circle; Fiskars
Die Cut letters: Accu-Cut
Font: DJ Inkers; Doodlers

Tip: The page idea is from the girl's outfit.

"You're My Hunny"
by Lana Rickabaugh of Maryville, MO

Black paper: Daisy D's
Yellow paper: Colorbok
Lettering template: Provo Craft
Font: CK Script
Stickers: Susan Branch

" 'The Park,' said Pooh..."
by Lana Rickabaugh of Maryville, MO

Stickers: Sandy Lion
Daisy punch: Marvy Unicha
Font: "Pooh" (of course) which came with the Pooh print studio
Pattern paper: unknown

"Park Day"
by Sherri Winstead of McChord AFB, WA

Grass Background Paper: Rocky Mountain Craft
Bottom park border: My Minds Eye
Tags: unknown
Boy stickers: Karen Foster
Chalk: Craf-T
Red Eyelets
Lettering template: Deja Views; Spunky 1"

Tip: Handcut lettering from left over leaf pictures, then tore green cardstock for a border on the bottom. Then, cut again on black cardstock.

"Dirt"
By Jeanette Brinkerhoff of Salt Lake City, UT

Patterned paper: Provo Craft
Cardstock: blue, brown, gray, black
Lettering templates: Deja Views; Spunky 2
Pens: Zig Writer and Gel Pens
Shovels: own design
Wheelbarrow: Adapted from a Provo Craft template

Tip: I wet the brown cardstock then scratched it up with a wire brush to give it more of rough texture.

"My House"
by Lana Rickabaugh of Maryville, MO

Paper: Provo Craft
Lettering template: Provo Craft Blocky
Font: Cool dots
Pop dots: All Night Media

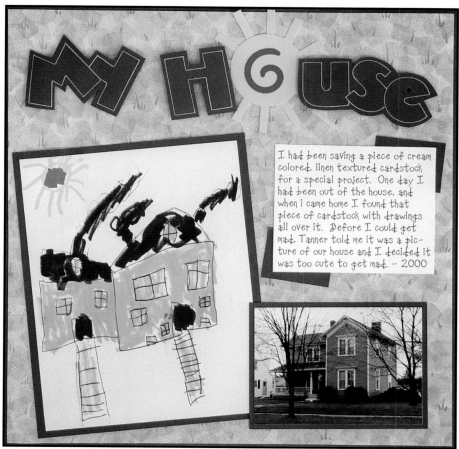

Children

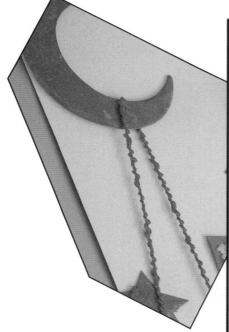

"Washin Me"
by Briana Dziekan of Milford, MI

Purple cardstock and pinkish/white cardstock for the title: Provo Craft stickers
Patterned paper: MMI Colors by Design
Pen: White Gel pen
Title: Shapemakers Coluzzle template

"Dream Catcher"
by Natahsa Roe of Sebring, FL

Pen: Zig Writer
Chalk: unknown
Rusty shapes: Provo Craft
On The Surface Fibers

"Cowboy Cousins"
by Dee Gallimore Perry of Griswold, CT

Font: Western; from internet
Journaling: CK Handprint
Letter stickers: Colorbok; David Walker
Cut outs: Cock-A-Doodle Design
Pen: Zig Millennium
Chalk: Craf-T Products
Jute

Brendan and Lauren had a great time playing Cowboys! All's they needed was their hats and their guns...(oh, and a horse) and they were all set! I stopped them long enough to take a few pictures...then off they went!

April 2000

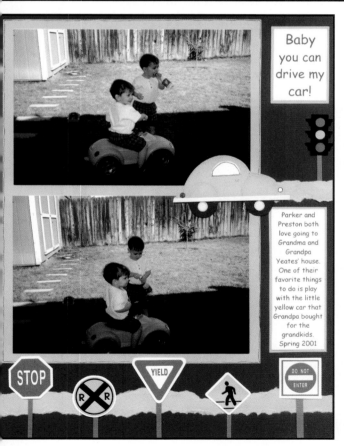

Baby you can drive my car!

Parker and Preston both love going to Grandma and Grandpa Yeates' house. One of their favorite things to do is play with the little yellow car that Grandpa bought for the grandkids. Spring 2001

STOP
YIELD
DO NOT ENTER

"Baby You Can Drive My Car"
by Jeanette Brinkerhoff of Salt Lake City, UT

Cardstock: navy, dk yellow, white
Fonts: Comic Sans
Stickers: Frances Meyer
Paper piecing: Car-adapted from a diecut

"I'm A Pepper"
by Jeanette Brinkerhoff of Salt Lake City, UT

Cardstock: black, white, dk. red
Lettering templates: Deja Views; Spunky 2

Tip: I pop dotted two of the letters in the title for visual interest. I also included the lyrics from the old Dr. Pepper commercial in the matt around the photo.

"Pepperoni"
by Lana Rickabaugh of Maryville, MO

Font: Beeswax
Journaling: CK Script

Tip: Used pop dots on the title

"Yumm"
by Lana Rickabaugh of Maryville, MO

Stickers: Frances Meyer
Paper: Unknown
Font: Cool Dots

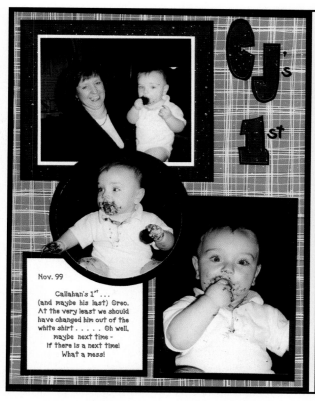

Nov. 99

Callahan's 1st . . .
(and maybe his last) Oreo.
At the very least we should
have changed him out of the
white shirt . . . . . Oh well,
maybe next time -
if there is a next time!
What a mess!

"Oreo"
by Jennifer Blackham of West Jordan, UT

Paper: The Robin's Nest
Journaling font: DJ Chunky
Title font: Expert Software; Jiffy
Letter stickers: Provo Craft

"Cute To The Core"
by Lana Rickabaugh of Maryville, MO

Paper: Northern Spy
Lettering template: Provo Craft; Blocky

Children

"A Boy Is Joy"
by Sherri Winstead of McChord AFB, WA

Freshcuts: Bumpercrops
Background paper: Rocky Mountain Scrapbook
Cardstock: Pebbles

"Buddies"
*by Sherri Winstead of
McChord AFB, WA*

Pattern paper: Paper Fever
Die cuts: My Minds Eye
Frame UP Friends
Blue Wire
Blue buttons: Hillcreek
Designs
Red heart button: Hillcreek
Fonts: Think Small and
Think Tall
(www.twopeasinabucket.com)

Tip: The border idea came
from Becky Higgins's
Creative Companion Book
and the poem from
www.twopeasinabucket.com

"Box Boys"
by Sherri Winstead of McChord AFB, WA

Font: Lettering Delights Mixed and CK Slice
Paperkins: EK Success - hand cut the clothes to match the picture.
Pattern Paper: Lasting Impressions

Tip: I hand cut the box and added pop dots under the "lid" so that it would pop up and look dimensional.

I heard Matthew and Seth playing in the kitchen. When I went to see what all the fun was about, I saw them both in a box we had next to the trash can. They were laughing and having a grand time together. They were being so silly and yet so fun. Oh, the moments of childhood.

Boys in a BOX

"Best Buds"
by Heidi Steenblik of Salt Lake City, UT

Green and purple slush Paper: Carolee's Creations
Daisy cut outs: The Beary Patch
Title font: CK Flower Garden
Journaling font: CK Primary
Colored Pencils: Prismacolor; Berol
Purple Gel Pen: Milky Gel Pens
Chalk: Craf-T Products
Corner slot punch: Family Treasures

Best Buds

I just love these pictures of KaCee, Teri, and Stanley. I had just gotten my camera for my birthday, and was eager to try it out. So I gathered up the kids, and we all went outside to play. The kids started running around and turning somersaults in the grass. Stanley loved having his picture taken, and was making the cutest faces for me! When these three are in the right mood, they are the best of friends. They love to watch movies together, have sleepovers in each others' rooms, play Nintendo and computer games together, and just be goofy kids!

Children

"Up Close and Personal"
by Jenna Robertson of Henderson, NV

Patterned paper: O'Scraps
Cardstock: unknown
"and personal" font: CAC Pinafore

"On The Mend"
by Traci Johnson of Mesa, AZ

Paperdoll: PaperKins; EK Success
(I changed the cast to match my sister's in the photo)
Topper: Current
Decorative paper: Frances Meyer
Pen: Zig; .5 Black Writer
Punch: Family Treasures

"Sweetie"
by Kiyoko Walkenhorst of Bluffdale, UT

Die cuts: Heartland Paper
Letter die cuts: Ellison
Patterned paper: unknown

"Giggles and Grins"
by Kiyoko Walkenhorst of Bluffdale, UT

Font: Girls Are Weird; downloaded from internet
Bows: from a pre-printed photo frame
Paper and frames: Scrap In A Snap

I love this photo of my Kelsey all wet and tousled from the sprinkler, showing off her third lost tooth of the summer! August 1998

"Snips and Snails"
by Melanie Runsick of Swifton, AR

Cardstock: DMD Industries
Font: CK Delight
Jute: Crafts Etc.

Ships and snails and puppy dog tails...

Summer 2000

"What A Joyful Sound"
by Melanie Runsick of Swifton, AR

All cardstock: Bazzill
Patterned paper: Karen Foster
Buttons: Dress It Up
Title font: CK- Leafy Capitals
Journaling font: unknown
Jute: Crafts Etc.

"Little Boys Are Angels Too"
by Catherine Allan of Twin Falls, ID

Patterned paper: unknown
Lettering template: Pebbles in my Pocket; Block 1 1/4"
Vellum: unknown
Star punches: Marvy Uchida
Chalk: Craf-T
Eyelets: Impress Rubber Stamps
Paper piecing: Adapted from Windows of Time
Computer font: CK Jot
Poem from 2 Peas in a Bucket.com

"Jessica"
by Kiyoko Walkenhorst of Bluffdale, UT

All Products Scrap In A Snap

"Angels"
by Jeanette Brinkerhoff of Salt Lake City, UT

Patterned paper: unknown
Cardstock: Kraft, Wine
Lettering templates: PC Fancy Block
Pens: Zig Writer, Gel Pens
Fonts: By hand

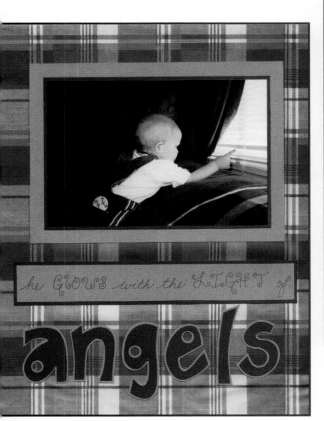

"Kelsey"
by Kiyoko Walkenhorst of Bluffdale, UT

All Products Scrap In A Snap

Children

"Cousins"
*by Anita Denson of
Decatur, AL*

Paper and Font:
unknown

"Tierney"
by Kiyoko Walkenhorst of Bluffdale, UT

Paper: KMA

Tip: Fabric was run through Xyron and adhered to
cardstock, cut and matted to form accent squares.

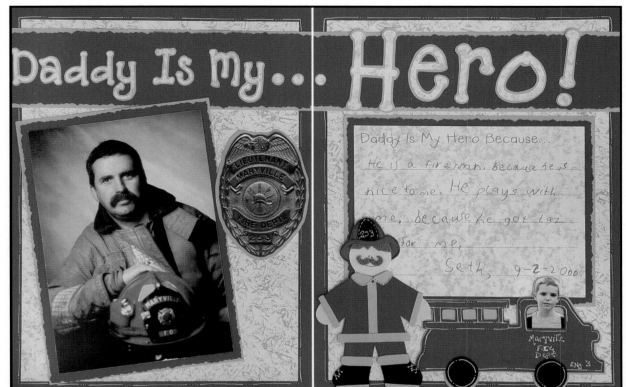

"Daddy Is My Hero"
by Lana Rickabaugh of Maryville, MO

Pattern paper: unknown
Scissors: Fiskars Deckle
Fonts: Cool Dots, CK Journaling

"Just You and Me, Kid"
by Kiyoko Walkenhorst of Bluffdale, UT

Letter stickers: Provo Craft Alphabitties
Dragonfly paper: Scrap In A Snap
Green paper: Carolee's Creations

Tip: Dragonfly was cut from paper and adhered with a pop dot for dimension.

**"Me and M[...]
Daddy"**
*by Kristen Swain[...]
Bear, DE*

Font: CK Flair, [...]
Penman
Color Pencils:
Prismacolor
Patterned pape[...]
KMA
Bows: Wallies[...]

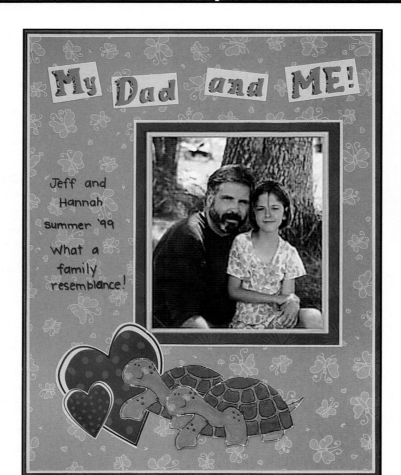

"My Daddy and Me"
by Kiyoko Walkenhorst of Bluffdale, UT

All products: Scrap In A Snap

"Motherhood"
by Vivian Smith of Calgary Canada

Paper: Provo Craft (purple fabric paper) Canford (gold)
Font: Loki Cola, downloaded from internet
Beautiful Ink, downloaded from internet
PC Stone Script, Provo Craft hugware "Little Images"
PC Fancy, Provo Craft hugware "Peeking thru the Garden Gate"

PC Script, Provo Craft hugware "For Font Sakes"
Libby Script, downloaded from the internet
Flower Punches: Family Treasures
Brads: Prime Media

"Still My Little Girl"
by Briana Dziekan of Milford, MI

Paper: Over the Moon Press
Cardstock: red and orange
Die cuts: unknown
Alphabet template: EZ2Cut

Friends/Family

"Brothers - Friends"
by Catherine Allan of Twin Falls, ID

Patterned paper: unknown
Heart template: Provo Craft; Happy Everything
Lettering template: Pebbles In My Pocket; Rounded 1 1/4 "
Vellum: unknown
Computer font: CK
Journaling from the Art of Creative Lettering CD's
Other: jute, buttons

Ribbon, beads, and string: Offray
Concho jewelry piece: American Craft
Punches: Family Treasures
Decorative paper: Keeping Memories Alive
Pen: Zig; Writer .5
Letter stickers: Frances Meyer
Silver decorative corners: 3L

"Sisters...Then and Now"
by Traci Johnson of Mesa, AZ

"Sisters"
by Jenna Robertson of Henderson, NV

cardstock: unknown
Title Font: Cute from "Kids"
Pooh and Piglet paper pieced.
Tip: A computer graphics program was used to put the girls in a storybook picture.

"Chattin' With Grandma"
by Jeanette Brinkerhoff of Salt Lake City, UT

Paper: unknown
Cardstock: White, Red
Title templates: Provo Craft Scrapbook 1
Pens: Zig Writer; Black
Other- Raffia

"Visiting Grandma"
by Traci Johnson of Mesa, AZ

Ribbons: Offray
Decorative paper: Keeping Memories Alive
Decorative scissors: Fiskars
Corner slot punch: Family Treasures
Lettering template: EK Success
Oval cutter: Creative Memories
Pen: Zig .5 Clean Color gray

Tip: I used a weaving technique to add the dark green ribbon to the cardstock- cut 2 slits 1/4" apart, spaced evenly every 1"; the light green bows are tied first, then glued on top.

"Grandma Annie"
by Heidi Steenblik of Salt Lake City, UT

Purple plaid paper: Karen Foster Design
Glittery Mulberry Paper: Print works
Title Font: CK Concave
Journaling font: CK Bella
Silver Glitter Pen: American Crafts
Punches: Heart; Emaginations, 1/16" hole: Fiskars
Floss: DMC #3041
Decorative scissors: Provo Craft

"Hanging Out With Papa"
by Sherri Winstead of McChord AFB, WA

Pattern paper: Karen Foster
Font: Provo Craft Nature
Buttons: Dress it Up
Jute

"Friends"
by Jeanette Brinkerhoff of Salt Lake City, UT

Patterned paper: KMA; Red Tweed
Cardstock: blue, kraft, cream
Title Templates: ABC Tracers; Varsity Upper
Pens: Zig Writer; navy, red
Other- jute

"Heather and Courtney"
by Heidi Steenblik of Salt Lake City, UT

Pink gingham paper: Jenny Faw Designs
Pink flower vellum: Printworks
Frame and heart die cut: O Scrap, Emaginations
Lettering template: Provo Craft; Blocky
Decorative scissors: Provo Craft Paper Shapers
Pens: American Crafts (white), Zig (all other colors)

"Friends Make Life Wonderful"
by Sherri Winstead of McChord AFB, WA

Font: CK Flower Garden
Pattern paper: Autumn Leaves
Pattern paper for pots: Provo Craft Itty Bitty Scrap pad
Punchart: Martha Stewart; Ash punch, All Night Media; mini flower and
mini circle, Fiskars; hand held circle punch, EK Success; Paper Shapers
(grass, pom pom, and tri-leaf punch)
Adhesive for punch art: Xyron 500

"Families Are Tied With Heart Strings"
by Jeanette Brinkerhoff of Salt Lake City, UT

Cardstock: navy, burgundy, green
Computer font: Angelica
Stickers: Provo Craft
Other: jute

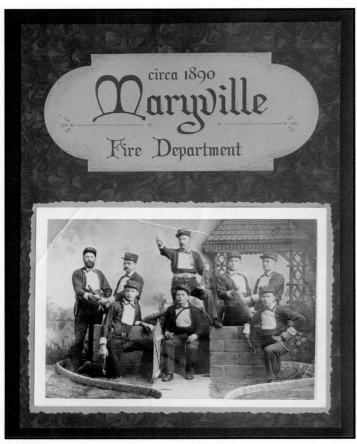

"Maryville Fire Department"
by Lana Rickabaugh of Maryville, MO

Scissors: Fiskars Deckle
Paper: Hot off the Press
Font: Unknown

"The Wedding Party"
by Heidi Steenblik of Salt Lake City, UT

Patterned Paper: Carolee's Creation; tan, Northern Spy; pink
Vellum: XPEDX
Page toppers: Cock-A-Doodle Design
Punches: All Night Media and Family Treasures
Title font: CK Wedding
Pen: Zig

"Jason & Caroline"
by Briana Dziekan of Milford, MI

Paper: Anne Griffin
Cardstock: Green
Stickers: MAMBI
ABC stickers: David Walker
Gold cording

"Bride's Maid"
by Briana Dziekan of Milford, MI

Cardstock: Green and purple
Pattern paper: MM Colors by Design
Flower stickers: Debbie Mumm
Letter template: Accucut
Pen: Zig

"Imagine"
by Lana Rickabaugh of Maryville, MO

All paper and vellum: K & Company
Stickers: K & Company
Font: CK Script
Eyelets and pop dots

"Hiking Buds"
by Cindy Harris of Brentwood, CA

Pattern paper: Pixie Press
Cardstock: Making Memories
Raffia: Darice
Wood frame & branches: Beary Patch Cut-Outs
Lettering template: Serif by Scrap Pagerz
Leaf punch: Emaginations

"Nature Hike"
by Traci Johnson of Mesa, AZ

Circle cutter: Creative Memories
Title and cut-outs: The Beary Patch
Decorative scissors: Fiskars
Small flower punch: Family Treasures
1/8" circle punch: McGill
Decorative corners: 3L
Pens: Zig .5 black Writer and .01 black Millennium

The view was amazing from our vantage point on the edge of the Mogollon Rim!

July 1999

"Great Outdoors"

by Catherine Allan of Twin Falls, ID

Patterned paper: Over the Moon
Tree die cut: unknown
Tree punch: McGill
Page topper: Cock a Doodle Design
Computer font: CK Print from Creating Keepsakes Art of Creative Lettering CD's

"Ashley National Forest"

by Lana Rickabaugh of Maryville, MO

Trees: Carolee's Creations
Paper: Carolee's Creations
Font: DJ Jenn Pen
Pens: Tombo
Chalk: Craf-T
Fire helmet: My own design

"Riverbend Gardens"
by Briana Dziekan of Milford, MI

Background paper: Clubscrap
Torn paper cattails: own design
Alphabet template: Accucut.

"Rocky Mountain High"
by Lana Rickabaugh of Maryville, MO

Paper: Provo Craft
Frames: Ellison
Tree die cuts: Heartland paper
Journaling font: CK Journaling
Title: Coluzzle Templates
Chalk: Craf-T

Nature

"Nature Walk"
by Sherri Winstead of McChord AFB, WA

Embellishments: Bumpercrops; Freshcuts
Fibers: On the Surface
Cardstock: Pebbles

"Nature Boy"
by Sherri Winstead of McChord AFB, WA

Title block and embellishments: Pagerz Extraz
Pattern paper: Magenta
Leaves: Black ink
Adhesive: Crafters Pick Memory Mount Glue, Hermafix Tab Adhesives

"Matthew was so cute in the grass just posing with nature!"

"It's A Boy's Life"
by Sherri Winstead of McChord AFB, WA

Title and embellishments: Pagerz Extraz
Spring meadows and straw speckles: Judikins
Diamond glaze - used to adhere the speckles to the bottom of the page

My parents love going for walks. They especially like going for walks at the cabin & have convinced me to go along more than once. Although I just love the fresh smells & nature feel, I'm really not a big walker or hiker. Luckily, I am usually glad I went after the walk is over. This winter, Dad & Mom walked down to the lake, (about a 25min walk) & Dad had a bad fall. He slipped on some ice on the road & landed on his cheek-bone! Yikes! It resulted in 5 fractures along his cheek and brow bone & a sizeable piece of bone actually detached & compressed inwards about 8mm. They had to go home that night & the following day he had two metal plates & several pins inserted in his cheek. They made a 4" incision between his cheek and gum, one above his ear, and one along his eyebrow to complete the operation. Amazingly, Dad had very little bruising, & recovered quite quickly.

"Walkin' in the Wilds"
by Vivian Smith of Calgary Canada

Paper: Karen Foster (plaid) Carolee's Creations (background)
Font: PC Beach Front, Provo Craft hugware "Little Images"
Brads: Primemedia
Circle cutter: Provo Craft Circle Coluzzle
Egg punch: EK Success
Water color pencils: Prisma color
Title and stems: own design

Nature

"Cedar Breaks"
by Heidi Steenblik
Salt Lake City, UT

Lettering template:
Provo Craft
Tree template: Provo
Craft
Punches:
Emagination; heart,
Fiskars; holes
Pens: Zig Writer

Tip: I used scraps from
the photographs to create
the title. Also, I used a wet
Q-tip and ruler to trace the
edge of the journaling box.
Interestingly, the top layer
of cardstock tore straight
and the bottom layer didn't.
This was mounted on
green cardstock.

"Balanced Rock"
by Michelle Tardie of
Richmond, VA

Letter template: EK Success; School ABC Tracer
Eyelets: Impress Rubber Stamps
Green cardstock
Rocks: Hand cut and chalked
Journaling font: Cock-A-Doodle Design
Paper doll: Cock-A-Doodle Design

"Nature Girl"
by Heidi Steenblik of Salt Lake City, UT

Yellow gingham paper: Deborah Designs
Colored pencils: Prismacolor
Pen: Zig Writer
Leaves & flowers template: Provo Craft Micro templates
Hole punch: Fiskars
Chalk: Craf-T Products

"Catch of the Day"
by Lana Rickabaugh of Maryville, MO

Paper: Unknown
Font: DJ Squirrelly
Template: Provo Craft Blocky

"Charter Boat Fishing"
by Briana Dziekan of Milford, MI

Cardstock: blue and brown
Die cuts: O'scrap
Brown cardstock quilling and fish designs: own design
Title letters: Making Memories and Scrapotamus
Background paper: Carolee's Creations
Wire: Club Scrap (used to hold fish and lure)
Pop dots: unknown

"Saddle Up"
by Briana Dziekan of Milford, MI

Paper piecing: Bumper Crops
Cardstock: brown and blue
Letter template: Accu-cut

"Hoedown"
by Traci Johnson of Mesa, AZ

Doll patterns: Mom and Me Dolls
Corrugated paper: DMD Industries
Letter template: Provo Craft
Bow punch: Family Treasures
Chalk: Crayola
Pens: Zig .5 black Writer and Zig .1 Millennium; Pentel
Milky white gel
Raffia: AmTwist

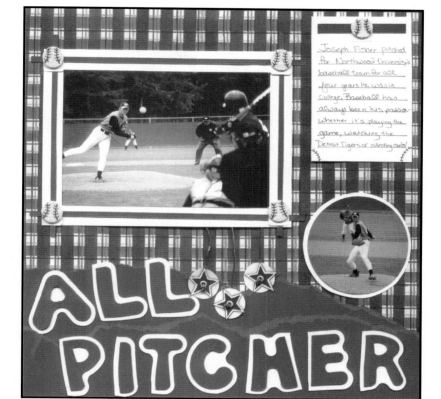

"All Star Pitcher"
by Briana Dziekan of Milford, MI

Cardstock: blue and white
Stickers: Jolee's boutique
Pen: Zig; red
Template: EZ 2 Cut
Gold cord: Fibre Craft
Eyelets: unknown
Star stickers: Sandylion
Paper: Bo-Bunny Press

Summer 1996
Seth is up to bat while playing T-ball. He loved spending summers practicing and playing ball. He looks so little with his extra large t-shirt and helmet on.

"Batter Up"
by Lana Rickabaugh of Maryville, MO

Font: CK Journaling
Header & footer: Overalls

"How I Play Golf"
by Lora Washburn of Killeen, TX

Cardstock: DMD Industries
Navy paper: unknown
Golf ball diecut: My Mind's Eye
Golf Bag diecut: unknown
Pens: Zig; Millennium, Zebra; Metallic Ink Gel Rollers

Tip: Torn background made using Xyron 850 to apply adhesive to torn strips.

"Let's Go Bowling"
by Natasha Roe of Sebring, FL

Letter stickers: David Walker
Bowling ball die cuts: Kangaroo & Joey

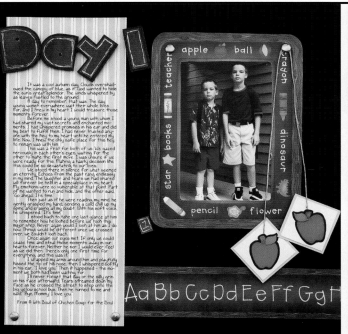

"Day 1"
by Lana Rickabaugh of Maryville, MO

Font: DJ Jenn Pen
Lettering template: Provo Craft Blocky
Frame and accents: Beary Patch
Gel pen: Marvy
Paper: unknown

"Kindergarten Graduation"
by Jennifer Blackham of West Jordan, UT

Font: DJ Crayon
Wood paper: Provo Craft
Paper piecing: based on a stamp by DOTS

First Day of preschool

Alizabeth started preschool at the YMCA sponsored school at the Salem United Methodist church on october 30, 2001. I was expecting her to be upset at being left alone in a new place with strangers, but she surprised us and had a wonderful time her first day. when I picked her up, her teacher told me that she had already made friends and many of the children were calling her to come play with them.

"First D.
of Pre·
school"
by Kristen S·
of Bear, D·

Paper: Pape·
Patch
Template: Sc·
Pagerz; Wate·
melon
Pen: Zig; Bla·
Apple punch·
McGill
Heart punch: F·
Shaper
Font: Scrap B·
Jute

Back to class

August 2000 Seth + Tanner get ready for their first Day of school. Seth is in fourth and Tanner starts his first day of all day Kindergarten. He's not happy about it either!

Seth Age 10
TaNNer Age 5

"Back To Class"
by Lana Rickabaugh of Maryville, MO

Header & footer: Overalls
Journaling block: My Minds Eye
Apple sticker: Mrs. Grossman
Paper: Unknown

"New York Harbor"
by Heidi Steenblik of Salt Lake City, UT

Lettering template: Provo Craft, Blocky
1/8" Hole Punch: Fiskars
Black photo corners: Canson
Journaling font: CK Penman
Pens: American Crafts and Zig

Tip: I drew the harbor scene in the title and accented with brush markers. I used an X-Acto Knife to silhouette my panoramic photos of the skyline to use as borders.

Journaling from the layout:

It was such a hot, muggy day, everybody went through about three bottles of water a piece! It was really great of Nanny and Grandpa Quack to take Dan and me everywhere in such weather. We took pictures on the ferry and out on Ellis Island against the New York City skyline. It was so cool to me to see it in person. It looked so big and small at the same time, I couldn't believe there was so much crammed into such a tiny space.

new york **Harbor**
july 6, 1999

We were heading back from the Statue of Liberty right about 5:00, and all of a sudden, there were a million sailboats in the harbor! I got this great picture of Dan and the sailboats at Liberty Park in New Jersey while we were waiting for Grandpa to get the car.

"The Side-walks of New York"
by Heidi Steenblik of Salt Lake City, UT

Skyline stickers: Frances Meyer
Title fonts: CK Contemporary
Journaling font: CK Penman
Pens: Zig Writers
Black photo corners: Canson

the **Sidewalks** of **New York**

After we ate our lunch in Times Square, we walked down 42nd Street to Fifth Avenue. Our first stop was the New York Public Library. It was really fun to see the Ghostbuster lions! From there, we continued up Fifth Avenue to the Rockefeller Center. I loved seeing the Prometheus statue, and where the skating rink and Christmas tree are in the winter. We didn't see the Radio City Music Hall, even though it was right there. We didn't know it was so close. It's okay, though, I've heard the Radio City Music Hall is depressing as hell.

From the cathedral, we walked further and saw Playboy Enterprises (I made Dan stop to get a picture), and the Trump Tower. The Tower was cool because it had trees growing in little parks on the side of the building.

We saw St. Patrick's Cathedral from the Atlas statue at the Rockefeller Center. We went in the cathedral to look around, but it was the middle of mass, so we didn't see much.

Image captions within San Francisco layout:
- world-famous clam chowder
- downtown view
- (in a sourdough bread bowl, of course!)
- Pier 39 & city
- Alcatraz view from pier
- docking slips for walruses & seals? Too cute!
- rolling blackout – CA. power crisis "crunch time"
- Sister shot

SAN FRANCISCO, CA.

"San Francisco"
by Traci Johnson of Mesa, AZ

Letter template: EK Success
Decorative paper: Current
Postcard: Smith Novelty Co.
Sun punch: Emagination
Other punches: Family Treasures
Corners: 3L
Pen: Pentel Milky white gel

"Seattle"
by Jami Blackham of Portland, OR

Letter template: Pebbles In My Pocket
Font: CK
Paper piecing: own design

Seattle

DECEMBER 4-7, 1998

WE HAD SUCH A GREAT TRIP TO SEATTLE. WE FLEW THROUGH THE MOST BEAUTIFUL SUNSET ON OUR FLIGHT THERE AND THE SKY WAS CLEAR AND STARRY WHEN WE ARRIVED FRIDAY NIGHT. THE CHRISTMAS LIGHTS WERE UP AND THE STREETS WERE BUSTLING WITH PEOPLE SHOPPING. OUR MOTEL HAD MUCH TO BE DESIRED, BUT WE WERE SO CLOSE TO ALL THE ACTION THAT WE COULDN'T COMPLAIN TOO MUCH.

WE ATE AT SOME FABULOUS RESTAURANTS—TWO THAT WERE IN THE FILM "SLEEPLESS IN SEATTLE." AND A COZY LITTLE ONE ON THE WATERFRONT CALLED SHEA'S LOUNGE.

SATURDAY MORNING WE WOKE UP TO RAIN, SO WE SOUGHT SHELTER INSIDE AT PIKE'S PLACE MARKET, THE SEATTLE AQUARIUM, AND OUR "CHARMING" MOTEL ROOM.

WE HAD A SUNNY, BUT COLD DAY ON SUNDAY WHEN WE WALKED TO THE SPACE NEEDLE FORR BRUNCH, TOOK THE MONORAIL BACK DOWNTOWN, AND THEN WALKED TO PIONEER SQUARE WHERE WE LOVED ELLIOT BOOKSTORE.

PHOTO GUIDE:
1. SATURDAY AT THE AQUARIUM
2. KOLBY BY PIKE'S PLACE
3. JAMI AT PIKE'S PLACE
4. JAMI ON TOP OF THE SPACE NEEDLE
5. KOLBY WITH SEA OTTERS AT THE AQUARIUM

MY FAVORITE PLACE IN SEATTLE WAS THE FARMER'S MARKET. PIKE'S PLACE IS JUST SUCH AN AMAZING SHOPPING ADVENTURE. THERE ARE SEVERAL FLOORS WITH ALL KINDS OF GOODS FOR SALE—PRODUCE, FRESH FISH, ARTS AND CRAFTS, BOOKS, COLLECTIBLES, CLOTHING. WHILE WE WERE SHOPPING WE BOUGHT FRESH FRUIT AND VEGETABLES TO SNACK ON. AND ON OUR LAST DAY THERE WE PICKED UP SOME FRESH CRAB TO TAKE HOME!

"Aloha"
by Lisa Goodman of Austin, TX

Cardstock: Paper Garden
Stickers: Creative Imaginations
Square punches: Family Treasures
Raffia: Paper Adventures
Corner lace punch: Emaginations; Arion
Lettering template: EK Success; Tracer -Block
Circle punch: Family Treasures
Computer journaling: DJ Inkers; Serif

"Tahiti Facts"
by Jami Blackham of Portland, OR

Font: Creating Keepsakes
Memorabilia pocket: 3L
Pencils: Prismacolor

"Key West Cruise"
by Briana Dziekan of Milford, MI

Title die cuts are chalked.
Mulberry paper is used under the boat.

"Tahquamenon Falls"
by Briana Dziekan of Milford, MI

Patterned paper: Provo Craft
Blue cardstock
Letter template: Coluzzle
Brown and black chalk
Computer font: Freehand 591 BT

"Bourbon St."
by Traci Johnson of Mesa, AZ

Decorative scissors: Fiskars
Letter template: Provo Craft
Circle punch and corner punches: Family Treasures
Pen: Zig .5 and 1.0 black Writer
Original paper piecing: I created

"Meramec Caverns"
by Briana Dziekan of Milford, MI

Cardstock: Brown and black
Postcards: Tickets from event
Title: ripped paper

Travel

"Jeepin' Arizona"
by Traci Johnson of Mesa, AZ

Letter stickers: Paper Adventures
Pen: Zig .5 black Writer
Die cut: Accu-Cut
Tip: I used the tear art technique to achieve the "sunset" background.

"Southwest Memory Expo"
by Traci Johnson of Mesa, AZ

Computer font: Corel; stagecoach
Eyelets American Craft
SW Memory Expo title: enlarged from my nametag from the expo
Oval cutter: Creative Memories
Border and decorative stickers: Stamping Station

"My Red Tiburon"
by Traci Johnson of Mesa, AZ

Decorative paper: NRN Designs
Die cut: Accu-Cut
Road: Frame Ups
Computer font: Corel; Submarine
Letter stickers: Provo Craft
Corner punch: Family Treasures
Chalk by Craf-T

"Animal Kingdom"
by Vivian Smith of Calgary Canada

Paper: Provo Craft
Circle punch: EK Success; Paper Shapers
Font: Bones; downloaded from internet
Provo Craft; Beach
Bamboo: own design

"Tree of Life"
by Dena Crow of Decatur, AL

Title: enlarged from a brochure
Tree: my own design
Stickers: unknown, purchased at Disney souvenir store

Theme Park

"Walt Disney World"
by Dena Crow of Decatur, AL

Title and "2001": enlarged from brochure
Pop dots: unknown
Pens: Creative Memories

Tip: I used an X-Acto knife to cut out the
background around the "2001".

"Character Parade"
by Dena Crow of Decatur, AL

Letter stickers: Creative Memories
Stamps: unknown
Pencils: Prismacolor

Grand and Christina waiting for
the parade to start.

Daniel & Christina dancing
with Aladin's helpers.

The Little Mermaid ~ John's favorite!

Daniel dancing in the parade!

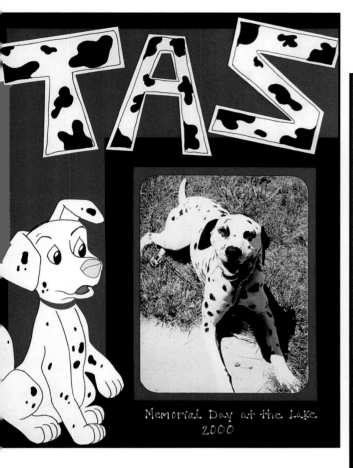

"Taz"
by Lana Rickabaugh of Maryville, MO

Letters: My own design
Dalmatian: made from a coloring book
Gel pen: Marvy

"Kitty, Kitty"
by Kiyoko Walkenhorst of Bluffdale, UT

Paper: Carolee's Creation
Daisy punch: Family Treasures
Letter stickers: DJ Inkers
Photo corners: unknown
Pen: Zig
Jute

"I Love My Kitten"
by Kiyoko Walkenhorst of Bluffdale, UT

Borders: Nag Posh, Trim It Up, velvet iron-ons
Lettering stencil: Provo Craft
Font: Tempus Sans

Pookie is...

Pookie likes:
~ sitting on the table
~ hiding behind the bathroom door
~ following Mommy around (and talking to me)
~ visiting "outside"
~ treats on the counter
~ ear scratchings

Pookie dislikes:
~ her dog
~ being picked up
~ baths

Summer 2000

"Pawsitivel Purrfect"
by Traci Johnson Mesa, AZ

Topper and cat cut o The Beary Patch
Velveteen paw pape Cache Junction
Circle cutter: Creati Memories
Punch: Family Treasures
Pen: Zig .5 black Wri
Decorative scissors Fiskars
Memory button: Elli

"Mack"
by Lana Rickabaugh of Maryville, MO
Paper and stickers: Susan Branch
Font: Sheer Grace

Mack
November
2000

Mack is the kitty that everyone would like to have for a pet! He is so sweet and loving. He expects his daily 'rubbins' and love pettings. He is Lana's little shadow, going everywhere that she goes!

LOVE

"Mack with Collar"
by Lana Rickabaugh of Maryville, MO

Scissors: Provo Craft Grass
Punch: Marvy Unicha
Title font: unknown
Paper: Susan Branch
Collar: a Christmas ornament

"Two days after we got Humphrey, we noticed an oozing abcess under his right ear. I called PetSmart to see what they could do, since he was still under the 14 day guarantee. The on-call manager told me that I could bring Humphrey in and exchange him for another pig. I told the manager that I wouldn't exchange him, and he said that I could take him to their vet and the store would pay for it. Dr. Shuck-Lee was a really great vet, she flushed the wound out, and gave me some antibiotic medicine for Humphrey to take orally twice a day. Humphrey loved it! Dr. Shuck-Lee had put a sweetener in the medicine so that he would take it more easily. We went back for a check-up in two weeks, and it was healed. After that, he started jumping around, and I thought he was having seizures! Then I found out that happy pigs love to jump around (it's called "popcorning") so he must have been feeling better!

"Vet Visit"
by Heidi Steenblik of Salt Lake City, UT

Patterned paper: Frances Meyer (Hospital)
Silver metallic paper: XPEEDX
Lettering template: Scrap Pagerz; Grade School
Journaling font: CK Curly
Stickers: Mrs. Grossman's , NRN Designs
Paper doll templates: Jill's Paper Doll World
Chalk: Craf-T Products
Pen: Zig Writer

"Leaping Lizards"
by Jennifer Blackham of West Jordan, UT

Font: CK Journaling
Tip: To create a matching accent for the page, I enlarged one of the lizards from the patterned paper and cut it out of cardstock.

- Leaping Lizards -

Red Butte Gardens
Summer 1999

Landon and Daddy

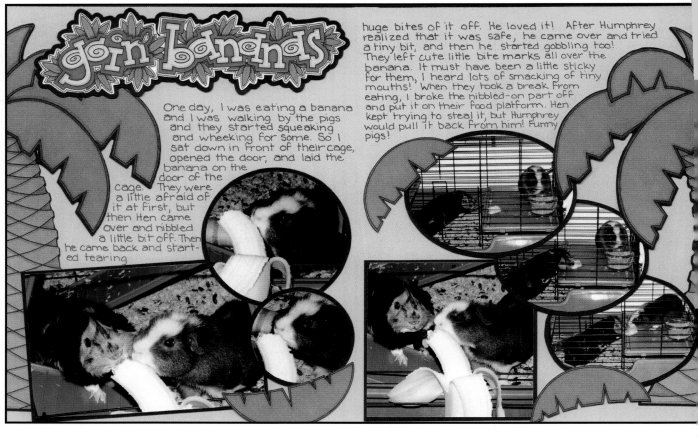

One day, I was eating a banana and I was walking by the pigs and they started squeaking and wheeking for some. So I sat down in front of their cage, opened the door, and laid the banana on the door of the cage. They were a little afraid of it at first, but then Hen came over and nibbled a little bit off. Then he came back and started tearing huge bites of it off. He loved it! After Humphrey realized that it was safe, he came over and tried a tiny bit, and then he started gobbling too! They left cute little bite marks all over the banana. It must have been a little sticky for them, I heard lots of smacking of tiny mouths! When they took a break from eating, I broke the nibbled-on part off and put it on their food platform. Hen kept trying to steal it, but Humphrey would pull it back from him! Funny pigs!

"Goin' Bananas"
by Heidi Steenblik of Salt Lake City, UT

Page topper and palm tree die cut: Cock-A-Doodle Design
Pen: Zig Writer

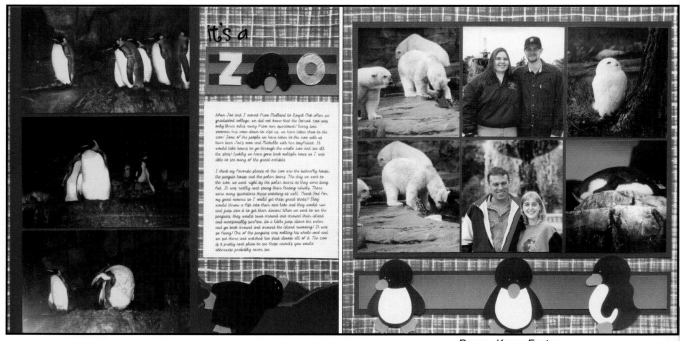

"It's A Zoo"
by Briana Dziekan of Milford, MI

Paper: Karen Foster
Blue cardstock
Silver paper
Penguins: own design
Stickers: David Walker and Stickopotamus
Vellum

California Dreamin'
by Linda Porter Jones of Long Beach, CA

Cardstock: Pebbles in My Pocket
Pen: ZIG Writer
Adhesive: ZIG 2-way Glue

"Steph"
by Linda Porter Jones of Long Beach, CA

Cardstock: Pebbles in My Pocket
Adhesive: ZIG 2-Way Glue

Mosaic

"Getting Ac-quainted"
by Cindy Harris of
Brentwood, CA

Cardstock & twistel: Making
Memories
Lettering template: Party by
Scrap Pagerz
Pens: The Ultimate White
Gel Pen and Zig Millennium

"Mosaic At the Spring"
by Jennifer Blackham of West Jordan, UT

Pen: Milky Gel Writer

Tip: A mosaic is an easy way to make a striking page. Use a metal ruler, X-Acto knife and a cutting mat to cut your squares. You could also use a paper cutter.

"My Little Hide-A-Way"
by Natasha Roe of Sebring, FL

Lettering: own design
Pen: Zig Writer
Patterned paper: unknown

Pencils: Prismacolor
Accents: Doodle Bug Designs
Eyelets: unknown

"Spa Day"
by Vivian Smith of Calgary Canada

Paper: Provo Craft; purple, yellow
Wintech; white puffy
Canford; gold
Lettering template: Provo Craft Puffy

Font: CK Journaling
Circle punch (earrings): Punch Line
Chalk: Craft-T
Paper doll: Stick People

Miscellaneous

"Housework Is Loads of Fun"
by Jenna Robertson of Henderson, NV

Paper and cardstock: unknown
Title: CK Lettering CD

"Texture"
by Kiyoko Walkenhorst of Bluffdale, UT

Pattern paper: Scrap In A Snap
Handmade texture paper: Carolee's Creations
Tool pattern: Bumper Crops
Silver paper: unknown
Letter template: Provo Craft Blocky
White pen: Pentel Milky Gel

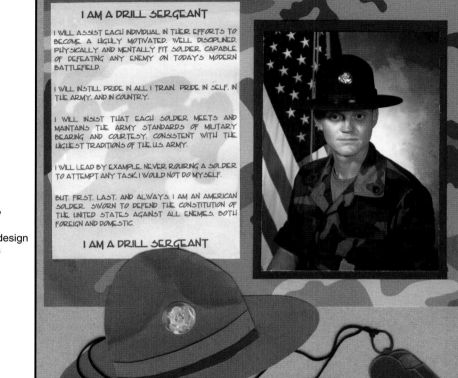

"I Am A Drill Sergeant"
by Lora Washburn of Killeen, TX

Cardstock: DMD industries
Camouflage paper: Frances Meyer
Vellum: DMD Industries
Computer journaling: The Print Shop; Enview
Black embroidery floss: DMC
Whistle and campaign hat paper-piecing: my own design
Adhesive for vellum: Fiskars clear photo tabs
Other adhesives: Hermafix tabs

"All The World's A Stage"
by Traci Johnson of Mesa, AZ

Topper and bottom: Current
Punch: Family Treasures
Photo corners: 3L
Computer font: Corel "Alegro"
Oval cutter: Creative Memories

Notes: